BEING FEMALE IN AMERICA

SEXISM IN THE MEDIA

BY DUCHESS HARRIS, JD, PHD

Essential Library

An Imprint of Abdo Publishing | abdopublishing.com

ABDOPUBLISHING.COM

Published by Abdo Publishing, a division of ABDO, PO Box 398166, Minneapolis, Minnesota 55439. Copyright © 2018 by Abdo Consulting Group, Inc. International copyrights reserved in all countries. No part of this book may be reproduced in any form without written permission from the publisher. Essential Library™ is a trademark and logo of Abdo Publishing.

Printed in the United States of America, North Mankato, Minnesota
092017
012018

THIS BOOK CONTAINS
RECYCLED MATERIALS

Cover Photo: Shutterstock Images
Interior Photos: Harry How/Getty Images Sport/Getty Images, 4–5; Tamas Kovacs/ MTI/AP Images, 9; Dmytro Aksonov/iStockphoto, 13; Richard B. Levine/Newscom, 16–17; Richard Levine/Alamy, 19, 95; f4foto/Alamy, 21; Suntzulynn for LE/Splash News/Newscom, 27; Andrea Raffin/Shutterstock Images, 28–29; Featureflash Photo Agency/Shutterstock Images, 31; Mark Poprocki/Shutterstock Images, 36; Ian West/ PA Images/Alamy, 39; Lionel Hahn/Sipa USA/AP Images, 42, 46–47; Allstar Picture Library/Alamy, 44; Charles Sykes/Invision/AP Images, 52; iStockphoto, 54–55, 88–89, 93; Joseph Sohm/Shutterstock Images, 58; Bill Putnam/Zuma Wire/Zuma Press, Inc./ Alamy, 63; Eldar Nurkovic/Shutterstock Images, 66–67; Richard Drew/AP Images, 72–73; Shutterstock Images, 77; Selim Aksan/iStockphoto, 78; Andrey Popov/ iStockphoto, 80–81; RH Ingram_OG/Ingram Publishing/Alamy, 86; Atlaspix/Alamy, 98

Editor: Alyssa Krekelberg
Series Designer: Maggie Villaume
Contributor: Carla Mooney

PUBLISHER'S CATALOGING-IN-PUBLICATION DATA

Names: Harris, Duchess, author
Title: Sexism in the media / by Duchess Harris.
Description: Minneapolis, Minnesota : Abdo Publishing, 2018. | Series: Being female in America |
Identifiers: LCCN 2017946736 | ISBN 9781532113116 (lib.bdg.) | ISBN 9781532151996 (ebook)
Subjects: LCSH: Sexism--Juvenile literature. | Sexism in mass media--Juvenile literature. | Social history--Juvenile literature.
Classification: DDC 302.230--dc23
LC record available at https://lccn.loc.gov/2017946736

CONTENTS

SEXISM AT THE SUMMER OLYMPICS

At the 2016 Rio Summer Olympics, American athlete Corey Cogdell-Unrein won a bronze medal in women's trapshooting. This is an event in which athletes shoot at clay pigeons released from a spring trap. Cogdell-Unrein had been a competitive shooter for 15 years. She was also a three-time Olympic athlete. She had also won another bronze medal at the 2008 Summer Olympics in Beijing, China. Back in the United States in 2016, the *Chicago Tribune* tweeted this about her victory: "Wife of a Bears' lineman wins a bronze medal today in Rio Olympics."[1]

The newspaper's tweet immediately sparked outrage among fans and readers. They blasted the paper for leaving out Cogdell-Unrein's name and event but including her marriage to National Football League (NFL) player Mitch Unrein. Critics called the tweet another example of everyday sexism in the media. One reader tweeted, "It's a good thing she's married to a Bears lineman otherwise you [*Chicago Tribune*] might not have cared."[2] Another reader wrote on Twitter, "Congrats to that Bears lineman who apparently deserves all the credit here."[3] Even the accompanying article in the *Chicago Tribune* about Cogdell-Unrein's win focused heavily on her husband. The short article included details such as how the couple met and how Mitch Unrein could not attend the Olympics to cheer on his wife because of his commitment to the Bears' training camp.

Cogdell-Unrein did not believe the newspaper's tweet was intentional or malicious. "I just kind of thought, 'Well, you know, they probably could've chosen a better heading to alert people of my victory,'" she says.[4] She did, however, believe the media needed to do a better job of recognizing women's achievements. "I definitely understand that people want equality for women and that we should be recognized for our own accomplishments and attributes outside of who we're married to or what our husband[s] or significant others have accomplished," she says.[5]

Ultimately, the newspaper apologized for its coverage of Cogdell-Unrein's Olympic achievement. "In an initial tweet and headline, we identified three-time U.S. Olympian Corey Cogdell-Unrein only as the 'wife of a Bears lineman,'"

PRETTY PENNY

Sixteen-year-old Canadian swimming star Penny Oleksiak won four medals at the 2016 Rio Olympics: a gold in the 100-meter freestyle, a silver in the 100-meter butterfly, and two bronzes in the women's 4x100- and 4x200-meter freestyle relays. Yet when the *Toronto Sun* put her picture on the front page, it used a headline that referenced her appearance, "Pretty Penny," not her accomplishments.[6] And when Canadian sports reporter Ron MacLean interviewed Oleksiak, he turned the conversation from Oleksiak's accomplishments to her older brother in the National Hockey League (NHL). He played a video of Oleksiak's brother scoring his only NHL goal. MacLean even asked Oleksiak if her brother had told her stories about Jamie Benn, the captain of the NHL's Dallas Stars.

editors wrote. "She's awesome on her own. We focused too hard on trying to emphasize the local connection Cogdell-Unrein has to Chicago."[7]

THE "MAN RESPONSIBLE" FOR A GOLD MEDAL

The *Chicago Tribune*'s coverage of Cogdell-Unrein was only one example of a news outlet being criticized for its reporting on female athletes at the 2016 Rio Olympics. Hungarian swimmer Katinka Hosszu, nicknamed the "Iron Lady," swam an incredible race in the women's 400-meter individual medley. She won the gold medal and beat the event's world-record time by more than two seconds. Many people praised her performance as one of the best of the Rio Olympics.

Following Hosszu's victory, NBC News's television coverage showed Shane Tusup, Hosszu's husband and coach, as he wildly cheered. NBC commentator Dan Hicks described Tusup as the man responsible for her success. Viewers widely criticized NBC and Hicks for the comment, with many people complaining that the comment was sexist and did not properly give Hosszu credit for her athletic achievement.

In response to the outcry, Hicks insisted he was trying to show viewers an accurate picture of Hosszu and her husband. Hosszu has credited her husband with helping

Katinka Hosszu got her nickname after earning five medals in just two days at the 2012 World Cup in China.

her improve her training, confidence, and intensity in the pool. "It is impossible to tell Katinka's story accurately without giving appropriate credit to Shane, and that's what I was trying to do," says Hicks.[8] He does admit, however, that he could have more carefully chosen his words.

SEXISM AND THE OLYMPICS

In recent years, coverage of women's and men's Olympic events has been balanced. This is driven in part by the popularity of events in which American women have dominated, such as beach volleyball, gymnastics, swimming, diving, and track and field. According to a team of researchers who tracked coverage by gender, the 2016 Rio Olympics were no exception. In the first week of the 2016 Games, more than one-half of the television coverage included female athletes.

Yet even though they receive equal time, female Olympians are often treated differently by the media. Researchers from

WRITING IN HER DIARY

During NBC's coverage of women's gymnastics, commentator Al Trautwig observed Sanne Wevers, a gymnast from the Netherlands, writing in a notebook after she finished her balance beam routine. Trautwig commented on air that Wevers might be writing in her diary. Retired gymnast and Olympic analyst Nastia Liukin quickly corrected him. She explained that Wevers was most likely writing down and calculating her scores in the notebook.

Cambridge University Press studied the differences in how people talk about male and female Olympians. They also studied how their word choices may influence gender attitudes toward athletes. The researchers examined millions of words from news articles, Internet websites, social media, and other sources. They compiled the words used most often to describe men and women competing in the Olympics. For male athletes, language was more likely to focus on their sporting performance. Words such as *fastest, strong*, and *biggest* were commonly used to describe men. For females, language focused more on their appearance and personal lives. Commonly used to describe females were *unmarried* and *married,* as well as references to their age.

Marie Hardin, dean of the College of Communications at Penn State University, says reporting on female athletes at the Olympics was uneven. Some news stories highlighted the strong performances of female athletes and featured them accurately as competitive

#COVERTHEATHLETE

Using the hashtag #CoverTheAthlete, social media users called out reporters and media outlets for sexist Olympic commentary and coverage of female athletes. They demanded that the media focus on athletes' performances, not their appearance. The social media campaign began in 2015 after an Australian journalist asked Canadian tennis player Eugenie Bouchard to twirl and talk about her clothing. Viewers widely criticized the interview and called it sexist and condescending.

athletes. Yet in other instances, the media's sexist treatment of female Olympians still occurred. For example, American swimmer Katie Ledecky won four gold medals and one silver medal at the Rio Olympics. But she was said to "swim like a man."[9] In judo, Majlinda Kelmendi became Kosovo's first Olympic medalist in history when she defeated Odette Giuffrida from Italy. Yet BBC commentators described the intense gold medal final as a "cat fight."[10] And Team Great Britain rower Helen Glover was asked by the *Daily Mail* about her skin-care regimen and how her training routine affected her hair.

According to Hardin, the sexism found in the media's coverage of the Olympics can be blamed in part on how women are covered by the media outside the Olympics. "If we really want to entirely address the sexism that seeps into Olympic coverage, we need to take a hard look at how we do with coverage of female athletes between the Games. That's the much bigger issue. And I would argue that there is plenty of sexism there."[11]

COVERAGE OF WOMEN IN SPORTS

Outside of the Olympics, women's sports have never been more popular. Women are playing professional soccer, hockey, basketball, golf, tennis, and more. Thousands of women compete in college sports. Yet female athletes and

Sports networks are dominated by men's sports.

their sporting events are rarely featured in major news outlets and sports media.

SportsCenter is a well-known sports news show on the sports network ESPN. A recent 25-year longitudinal study on the coverage of women's sports on television found that female athletes were given minimal air time in 2014 on *SportsCenter*. The amount of air time had changed little from 1999, the year when the study started tracking *SportsCenter* in particular. "This is a persisting trend. It's just somewhat disappointing given the tremendous growth and participation in women's sports over the last 25 years

JUST A BASKETBALL PLAYER

Elena Delle Donne is a six-foot-five Women's National Basketball Association (WNBA) forward for the Chicago Sky. She was named the league's Rookie of the Year in 2013, and she was named Most Valuable Player (MVP) in 2015. In 2015, she hit 95 percent of her free throws.[14] Only three other players in history—male or female—have achieved this accomplishment. Delle Donne has been compared to LeBron James, Carmelo Anthony, and Kevin Durant. Yet she constantly deals with sexist comments from men. Some tell her they watch her play because she's good-looking. Others wonder why she is not in the kitchen.

in particular. That excitement is not being captured by the media," says Cheryl Cooky, associate professor of women's, gender, and sexuality studies at Purdue University and the study's coauthor.[12]

Some people argue that sports media are only providing audiences the stories they want to see. But Cooky disagrees. She says the interest in women's sports exists and points to the widespread enthusiasm for soccer's Women's World Cup in 2015. The USA-Australia match attracted more than three million viewers on Fox Sports 1, making it the largest audience ever for a soccer match on the channel.[13]

When women's sports are covered on the news, the media often handle them very differently than they do men's sports. In the 25-year television study, researchers found that news media such as *SportsCenter* often cover men's sports in a way that builds and engages audiences. They create a sense of excitement and provide colorful commentary to create engaging stories. When covering women's sports, however, the media coverage is less engaging, involves less storytelling, and is much more matter-of-fact.

SEXISM IN THE MEDIA

Sexism is the unfair discrimination against people because of their gender. In the media, sexism can occur in many forms. It can be found in the images used in advertising, the portrayal of female characters in movies and television, and the coverage of women in the news and in sports.

Many people have begun to stand up and speak out for the fair treatment of all people, regardless of gender. Understanding what sexism in the media is and how it appears is the first step toward creating a media industry that is fair and balanced in everything it covers.

DISCUSSION STARTERS

- How do you think a male athlete would react to being asked about his hair-care routine? Explain your answer.
- How often do you see coverage of women's sports on major news networks? Why do you think that is?
- How do you think the media can improve their coverage of women in sports?

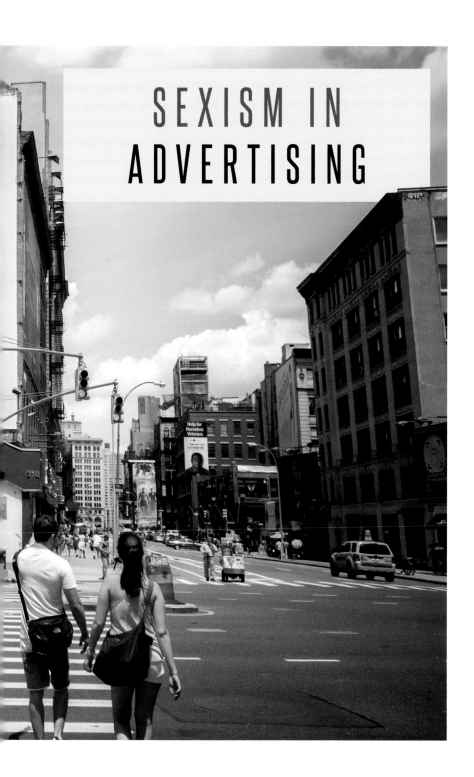

CHAPTER TWO

SEXISM IN ADVERTISING

In 2016, the fashion brand Calvin Klein launched a controversial advertising campaign that featured images of models and other celebrities wearing Calvin Klein underwear. The images were posted on the brand's Instagram account. Each image included a line about what the person in the picture liked to do in his or her Calvins. The brand came under fire, however, for the two images it selected from the campaign to display side by side on a New York billboard. One image was a head shot of rapper Fetty Wap, who "make[s] money" in his Calvins.[1] The other image featured actress Klara Kristin leaning back on a couch with her dress raised and her legs spread apart, with the caption that she "seduce[s]" in her Calvins.[2]

Heidi Zak, the chief executive officer (CEO) and cofounder of lingerie brand ThirdLove, was so upset by the billboard that she launched a campaign to have it removed. Zak argued the billboard highlighted gender stereotypes of men as the providers and women as sex objects. In a letter to Calvin Klein's CEO Steve Shiffman, Zak called on the company to remove the sexist and offensive billboard. "It's striking that almost a century after women won the right to vote, companies like yours are still propagating these offensive and outdated gender stereotypes: Men go to work and make money, while

Showing one part of a woman's body is a popular advertisement technique.

women are nothing more than sex objects," she wrote.[3] The brand eventually removed the billboard but cited its removal as part of a planned advertising rotation.

In 2016, companies including Calvin Klein spent billions of dollars on advertising around the world. This included traditional print, radio, and television ads, along with online ads on websites, social media, and other digital platforms. Every day, the average American adult is exposed to hundreds of ads. And these ads sell much more than products. They sell images, values, and societal concepts of success and worth.

OBJECTIFICATION OF WOMEN

In advertising, companies create print, online, and television ads using images they think will help sell their product or service. They choose images they believe will make their product appear superior to its competitors.

USING SEX TO SELL

They also make people believe using the product will make them happier. Often, these advertisements and the images used objectify women. Objectification is the act of treating a person as an object or a thing. Many of today's advertisements include images of young, attractive women in sexually suggestive positions or women happily doing housework. These images objectify women as either sex objects or submissive housewives.

Another way sexism surfaces in advertising is through dismemberment ads. These ads focus on only one part of the body, such as a woman's lips, legs, butt, breasts, or torso. Dismemberment ads encourage people to see a woman's body as a collection of individual pieces instead of a whole person. By breaking down a woman into pieces, these ads dehumanize women.

Additionally, this type of ad rarely shows a woman's head. This sends the message that having ideal body parts is more valuable than being intelligent or having a personality. "When images only show sexualized parts of bodies—breasts, hips and waists—and remove the head from those parts, we're indicating that those sexualized parts represent femininity," says Tomi-Ann Roberts, a psychology professor at Colorado College.[5]

CREATING A FALSE IDEAL

Some advertisements not only objectify women but also do so using a false ideal that is impossible to achieve in real life. By using Photoshop and other digital editing programs, the advertising industry has created its version of the perfect woman. Seen throughout ads, the perfect woman has long, smooth legs, a tiny waist, ample breasts, a rounded butt, radiant skin, and thick, silky hair. Her teeth are impeccably white, straight, and perfect, while her eyes dazzle with color and brightness. She is flawless, without a blemish or wrinkle.

When Photoshop is used to manipulate a woman's face, the changes can make the final image drastically different from how the woman actually appears.

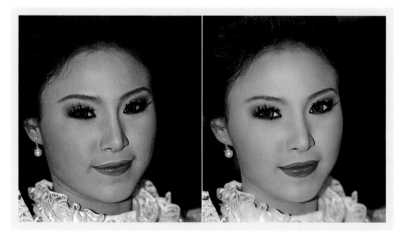

Yet the truth is that this woman does not exist in the real world. The advertising industry has created her through hours of work by professional hair and makeup stylists, flattering lighting, and days of photo editing and retouching. Professionals erase the blemishes on her chin. They color in the dark circles under her eyes. They nip in her waist and increase the size of her breasts, or digitally shave a few pounds off her hips.

The harm occurs when real women around the world compare themselves with advertising's false image of perfection. They buy products and strive to look like the women in advertisements, even if that is unrealistic. Comparing themselves with these ads often leaves women feeling bad about themselves. This can contribute to problems with body image and self-esteem.

USING REAL WOMEN IN ADS

Some brands have decided to stop using digitally altered and unrealistic images of women in their advertising campaigns. Instead, they are developing campaigns that feature women of all shapes, sizes, and ages. Beauty brand Dove launched the trend in 2004 when it introduced its Campaign for Real Beauty. The campaign featured normal-sized women who looked radiant without being digitally altered.

Aerie, a lingerie line from the clothing company American Eagle, is one brand that decided to stop airbrushing its models in 2014. Aerie's models will display tattoos, beauty marks, dimples, fat, and stretch marks just like real women. The company hopes this decision will help it promote more realistic beauty standards for its teen customers. "They are still models, they're still gorgeous,

DOVE'S EVOLUTION

In 2006, Dove released a time-lapse video titled "Evolution." The video showed how an average-looking woman is transformed into a breathtaking model using professional hair and makeup stylists, flattering lighting, and digital editing to lengthen her neck, smooth her skin, and enhance her eyes. The video pulled back the curtain on the manipulation advertisers use to create the flawless skin and breathtaking bodies often seen in ads.

they just look a little more like the rest of us," says Jenny Altman, an Aerie brand representative. "We're hoping to break the mold. . . . We hope by embracing this that real girls everywhere will start to embrace their own beauty."[6]

CREATING ADS THAT DO NOT OBJECTIFY

Some advertising professionals, including Madonna Badger, the founder of advertising agency Badger & Winters, are working to create ads that do not objectify women. In a 2016 pledge posted on its website and social media accounts, the agency made a commitment to never objectify women in its work. Badger and other advertising

#WOMENNOTOBJECTS

In 2016, advertising agency Badger & Winters created a two-minute video called #WomenNotObjects. In the video, models mock ads that feature barely dressed women in sexually suggestive positions for the purpose of selling food, clothing, and alcohol. In one segment, a woman mocks an ad for fast-food restaurant Carl's Jr., sarcastically saying she'd sell her body for a burger.

Some companies in the #WomenNotObjects video resisted acknowledging their ads as sexist and demeaning. Carl's Jr. noted that its models participated willingly in their ads. "The women in our award-winning ads are intelligent, talented and beautiful professional actresses and models who often reach out to us and voice their interest in being part of our fun, iconic ads. . . . We have only the greatest respect for women and their contributions to society at all levels in business, at home and in the community."[7]

executives say it is possible to create successful ads that do not objectify women, and there are more being made all the time. They hope to lead by example on this issue.

Some critics say that is more easily said than done. They point out that Badger herself was one of the creative minds behind several ads in the 1990s that objectified women. Badger explains that she has learned from past mistakes and believes the advertising industry is learning as well. Decades of research have shown that objectifying women in ads continues negative stereotypes for both women and men and is not well received by women. "Agencies create advertising that promotes not only the product, but also the people who make it.

Ads should never 'use people' or take advantage of women and men in any way, shape or form," Badger says.[8]

In recent years, the way women have been represented in ad campaigns has started to change. Some advertising professionals credit the power of social media with bringing about swift change. Through social media, individuals have the ability to talk back directly to brands and let them know in no uncertain terms what they think about a particular ad campaign. If a person finds an ad offensive or sexist, he or she can call out the brand immediately. And when millions of potential customers send negative feedback on an ad, some brands have started to listen.

DISCUSSION STARTERS

- Some people say there is a difference between celebrating beauty and objectifying women in advertising. What do you think they mean? Do you agree?
- Is there a difference in how dismemberment advertising is used for men versus women?
- Which brands do you think use realistic models and images in their ads? Which ads do you think are the most retouched? How can you tell?

MISS
REPRESENTATION

Released in 2011, *Miss Representation* is a documentary that explores gender bias and how women are depicted in the media as sex objects, as victims, and as short-tempered shrews. It was written and directed by filmmaker Jennifer Siebel Newsom. The documentary also explores how the media's portrayal of women has a harsh effect on how young women see themselves and how society views women in power. The film includes stories from teenage girls and interviews with politicians, journalists, entertainers, activists, and academics, such as Katie Couric, Rosario Dawson, Gloria Steinem, Margaret Cho, Condoleezza Rice, Rachel Maddow, and Nancy Pelosi. The film's underlying message is that young women need positive role models and the media has failed to provide them.

Newsom wants the film to be a catalyst to inspire and engage people to stand up for women's rights. In the film, an expert suggests that women should use their enormous purchasing power to support businesses that do not demean women. A young man talks about having the courage to speak up when others make sexist comments. Since its release, the film has sparked several movements to speak out against sexism in the media.

Posters promoting *Miss Representation* appeared in 2011.

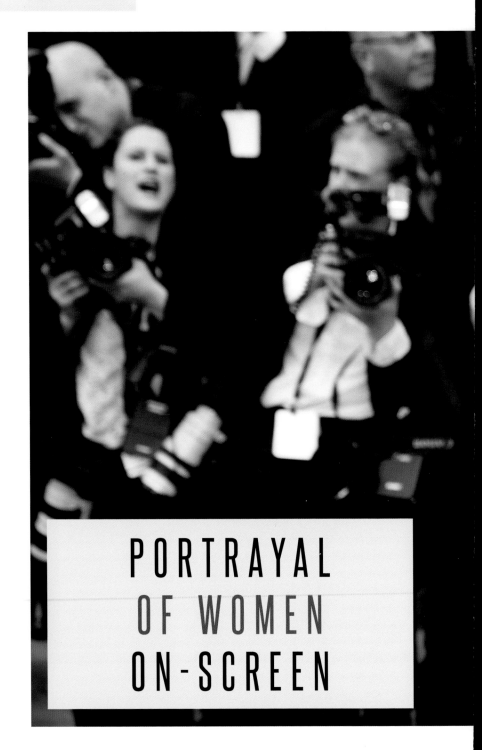

PORTRAYAL OF WOMEN ON-SCREEN

Women come in all shapes, sizes, and colors. They also come from many ethnic backgrounds. Women work in a wide variety of careers, as police officers, firefighters, doctors, lawyers, accountants, scientists, teachers, artists, entertainers, and more. They compete in athletics, volunteer to help those less fortunate, and nurture family and friends.

Movies and television can show audiences how the world currently exists, and perhaps even more important, how a better world could exist. Yet in many films and television shows, the world being shown is one in which women are underrepresented, rarely speak, and are often stereotyped.

UNDERREPRESENTED IN TELEVISION AND FILM

In 2016, the success of *Rogue One: A Star Wars Story* was powered by its strong female protagonist, Jyn Erso, played by actor Felicity Jones. The film ranked as one of the top-grossing films of the year. It received positive reviews from film critics and moviegoers alike. "We have now seen over and over and over that female characters, when done well, they're good [at the] box office," says Martha Lauzen, director of the Center for the Study of Women in Television and Film at San Diego State University.[1]

Yet despite the success of *Rogue One* and other films with female protagonists, women in film are often greatly underrepresented. According to a study by the Center for the Study of Women in Television and Film, the top

Felicity Jones played a dynamic female character in *Rogue One.*

100 US films in 2016 featured female protagonists only 29 percent of the time.[2] This percentage was an all-time high for female protagonists in film. In comparison, 54 percent of films had a male protagonist and 17 percent featured ensemble casts, in which a group of actors have roughly equal screen time and importance in the film.[3] In secondary roles, women are still underrepresented, making up 37 percent of main characters and only 32 percent of all speaking characters.[4] In fact, movie audiences in 2016 were more than twice as likely to see a male character on-screen as they were to see a female character.

Women of color were even more underrepresented in the top 100 US films. In 2016, the overwhelming majority of all female characters were white. Only 14 percent were African Americans. Asian, Latina, and other women of color fared even worse, appearing as 6 percent, 3 percent, and 1 percent of all female characters, respectively.[5]

On television, women did not fare much better. For the 2015–2016 television season, the Center for the Study of Women in Television and Film examined dramas, comedies, and reality shows that aired on network broadcast channels, cable channels, and streaming services. They found more than one-half of the broadcast, cable, and television programs featured more male than female characters in their casts. Five percent presented casts with equal numbers of female and male characters, while 16 percent of casts had more female than male characters. In addition, females were only 38 percent of major characters and 39 percent of all speaking characters across all television platforms.[6]

STEREOTYPES ABOUND ON-SCREEN

When women do make it on-screen, many movies and television shows present female characters that conform to gender stereotypes. They are typically less developed than characters played by their male costars. Female characters are often the girlfriend, wife, or mother of a male character. They are defined by their relationships to the male characters. In movies, male characters are more likely to have identifiable jobs. They are also more likely to be shown at work and actually working. Male characters also typically have identifiable work-related

SEXIST PORTRAYAL OF WOMEN

In 12 seasons on television, the hit show *Two and a Half Men* was well-known for its sexist portrayal of female characters. Regular female characters such as a main character's mother and ex-wife were stereotyped as selfish and awful. A neighbor girl was depicted as crazy. And most of the other women who appeared on the show were one-night stands for one of the main characters. These female characters were superficial and unintelligent. They rarely appeared in more than one episode.

goals. Female characters are more likely to have goals related to their personal lives, such as being in a romantic relationship or caring for others. Male characters are also more likely to be portrayed as leaders. "We're more likely to know the occupational status of men in film and we're more likely to know the marital status of women," says Lauzen.[7]

THE REAL HOUSEWIVES

The Real Housewives is a franchise of reality-television series broadcast on the Bravo cable channel. The shows document the lives of several affluent women living in various areas of the United States. Critics have complained that the shows present women in an extremely unflattering and stereotypical light. The shows focus on the women's appearances and social achievements. The women celebrate glittering jewelry and new clothing and spend most of their time on-screen gossiping and hosting parties. Many episodes emphasize the women's rude, mean, and backstabbing behaviors.

When female characters are shown at work, they are frequently missing from high-powered occupations. According to a 2014 study from the Media, Diversity, & Social Change Initiative at the University of Southern California (USC) Annenberg School for Communication and Journalism, less than 15 percent of business leaders, political figures, or science, technology, engineering, and math (STEM) employees on-screen were women in films released between 2010 and 2013.[8] Actress Geena Davis is the founder and chair of the Geena Davis Institute on Gender in Media. She believes movies and television have an important role in encouraging women to take these roles in real life and can change what the future will look like. "How do we encourage a lot more girls to pursue science, technology and engineering careers? By casting droves of women in STEM, politics, law and other professions today in movies," says Davis.[9]

When they do appear on-screen, female characters are often hypersexualized. They dress in sexy and revealing clothing, sometimes even appearing naked. According to a study of 2012 movies by researchers at USC Annenberg, 31 percent of women on-screen were shown with some exposed skin in the breast, midriff, or upper thigh area and nearly 32 percent wore sexually revealing clothing.[10] For teen characters, the hypersexualization was even more common. The majority of female teen characters wore revealing clothing in 2012 movies.

IT STARTS WITH A SCRIPT

In some cases, sexism on-screen begins even before the cameras start filming. Part of the problem can be found in the scripts that give actors their lines and set the stage for each scene. In television and movie scripts, female characters are often described primarily by how they look.

lack shoots a man in a co...
be on a Dumpster. and jumps
ase.

sprints down the alley with flashlight a...
and follows him through the warehouse wit...

OUSE - NIGHT

                    OFFICER
        Police! Drop your weapon and
        put your hands in the air!

                    MAN IN BLACK
        (Laughing) Do you really
        think you're going to stop me?

                    OFFICER
        Don't move, or I'll shoot!

                    MAN IN BLACK
        If you want me, come and get m

an in black disappears behind a tall r...
ders and cranks open a valve on one of
urized gas HISSES out.

... curses and looks for another
... forklift and jumps to a
... at the man in t

Hollywood film scripts have more men in lead roles than they do women.

In contrast, the descriptions of male characters focus more on their personality, character, and attitude.

Hollywood film producer Ross Putman says he has read thousands of scripts. And he's noticed a troubling pattern in the way female characters are introduced. Often, writers introduce female characters using descriptions such as leggy, attractive, blond, beautiful, hot, gorgeous, pretty, and sexy. Putman notes these descriptions don't add to the purpose of the script, and they don't help the actresses play the role. He points out that scriptwriters are much more likely to describe male characters by their personality, not just their appearance. Putman notes that the sexism in scripts is not limited to a select few writers. Instead, he has seen sexism in scripts by writers of all backgrounds, both professional and amateur.

To bring attention to the problem, Putman created a Twitter account on which he tweets the first description of a female character in an unproduced script, using the anonymous character name of Jane. One introduction reads, "Behind a steamy shower door is the indistinguishable but sexy silhouette of Jane showering." Another introduction describes Jane as "athletic but sexy. A natural beauty. Most days she wears jeans, and she makes them look good."[11] Putman says the reaction to his project has been overwhelming. His Twitter account has amassed thousands of followers. He hopes that, by highlighting the way women are described in scripts, he can help bring change and reduce sexism in Hollywood.

EVALUATING FEMALE REPRESENTATION

Some people use the Bechdel test as a quick way to evaluate female representation and gender inequality in works of fiction, including film and television. Popularized in the 1980s by writer and comic artist Allison Bechdel, the Bechdel test assesses works of fiction based on whether they meet three criteria: the work must have at least two women in it, the women must talk to each other, and they must talk about something other than a man. Some critics say the test is too simplistic and doesn't always work. "The ridiculously retrograde *Twilight*, for example, passes (doormat heroine, Bella, talks briefly to her mother about moving to a new town) while *Gravity*, which has a fierce, clever and interesting heroine, fails," writes feminist playwright Samantha Ellis.[12]

FINDING ROLES OF SUBSTANCE

Many female actors complain that it is difficult to find roles for women with substance and that offer complex, intelligent characters in a compelling plot. They also struggle to find roles that treat actresses as more than sexual objects or accessories to male leads. Actresses who want to challenge themselves in Oscar-caliber roles can rarely find scripts that would cast them as brilliant politicians, scientists, or adventurers. Instead, many of the roles offered to actresses are for supportive wives, sexy girlfriends, or uneducated women. At the 2016 Academy Awards, only three of the movies up for the Best Picture award featured women in the lead role: *Room*, *Brooklyn*, and *Mad Max: Fury Road*.

Frustration at the roles she was being offered led actress Reese Witherspoon to set up her own

Brie Larson won the 2016 Academy Award for Best Actress for her role in *Room*.

SEXISM IN CASTING

Actresses in Hollywood struggle with sexism even before they get on-screen. Sometimes, sexism emerges during the casting process. In 2016, actress Emmy Rossum received a call from her agent. She was excited to learn she was being offered a role in a big movie. Then her agent told her that in order to get the part, she would have to meet the film's director at his office, dressed in a bikini. The agent informed Rossum that she did not have to audition for the part, just wear the bikini. Rossum assumed the unusual request was because the role might involve her wearing a swimsuit, so she asked to see the film's script. There were no scenes that called for a swimsuit. Instead, Rossum realized the director just wanted to make sure she had not gotten fat. Rossum turned down the request and the role. She is concerned for younger actresses who might be more vulnerable and feel pressure to accept a similar sexist request.

production company, Pacific Standard, with partner Bruna Papandrea. Witherspoon says she had had enough of being offered below-standard, dumb-girlfriend-type roles. Once, she was sent a script and the film's producers told Witherspoon that three Oscar-winning actresses and two box-office-leading actresses were already competing for the part. "And I was like: 'Oh, that's where we're at? You're fighting to be the girlfriend in a dumb comedy? For what?'" she says.[13]

Since its creation, Pacific Standard has found success with films such as *Gone Girl* and *Wild*. Rosamund Pike, who played the female lead in *Gone Girl*, earned an Academy Award for best actress and a Golden Globe nomination for her role as a multilayered, missing woman. Witherspoon herself starred in *Wild* as a grieving hiker and earned nominations for best actress for both the Oscars and the Golden Globes.

Sexism on-screen in movies and television can have a lasting effect on audiences around the world. The way movies and television shows represent and portray women plays an important role in how women are seen and treated in society. By portraying women as equal partners and strong leaders, the entertainment industry can reduce sexism on-screen and promote gender equality to audiences worldwide.

DISCUSSION STARTERS

- What movies have you seen recently? Did they have male or female protagonists? How were male and female characters portrayed?
- What examples of sexism in television have you noticed?
- What female stereotypes have you noticed in movies and television?

SEXISM AND THE MUSIC INDUSTRY

In 2016, Björk, a singer-songwriter from Iceland, performed a DJ set at the Day for Night Arts Festival in Houston, Texas. She played and mixed recorded music selections. After her DJ performance, media critics wrote that she was "hiding" behind a desk instead of truly performing.[1] Several male artists at the event played similar sets. But they did not receive the same critiques. The unequal criticism sparked Björk to speak out publicly about her experience and others similar to it in the music

Björk recorded her first album when she was 11 years old.

industry. She wrote an open letter about the sexism she and other female artists face in the music industry. She posted it on her Facebook page.

In her open letter, Björk also talked about how the media treat female artists and the topics they choose to sing about. "Women in music are allowed to be singer songwriters singing about their boyfriends," she wrote. "If they change the subject matter to atoms, galaxies, activism, nerdy math beat editing or anything else than being performers singing about their loved ones they get criticized."[2]

DIFFERENT TREATMENT

There are many examples of the music media treating female artists differently than they do male artists. Many times, members of the media assume female artists cannot write or play music with the same ability as male musicians. Björk has had to correct journalists who assume she does not write her own music. Numerous female musicians have been asked if they were at the concert because they had a boyfriend in the band.

Sometimes, sexism in the music media can be more subtle. When journalists write about a woman in music, they often refer to her as a "female songwriter" or a "female guitarist." In contrast, when covering men in the industry, they are simply called songwriters or guitarists. "Including 'female' in front of our job description is differentiating us from our male counterparts, when we are doing the exact same thing as them, if not doing it better," says singer-songwriter Caroline Spence, who released her album *Spades and Roses* in 2017.[3] Spence argues that by labeling women as female first, they are being put at a disadvantage.

IMAGE AND BEAUTY

In newspapers, in magazines, and on websites, articles about male musicians rarely talk about their appearance or weight. Yet for female artists, articles often focus on how they look and what they are wearing. Sometimes, articles give these details priority over the woman's musical talent. In a 2015 *Vanity Fair* article, the writer opens her piece about Grammy-award-winning artist Rihanna with a description of what the singer-songwriter is wearing and her lack of makeup. With her first question, the

Although Rihanna has won eight Grammys, she continues to deal with comments focused on her appearance rather than her accomplishments.

journalist asks Rihanna how she keeps her slim but curvy figure. Then she launches into questions and a discussion about Rihanna's love life.

Women in music are also subject to body shaming if they do not meet certain ideals for beauty. Since the birth of her first child in 2014, Grammy-award-winner Kelly Clarkson has dealt with the media's negative comments about her weight. In 2015, Fox News's Chris Wallace commented that while Clarkson had a great voice, she should stay away from deep-dish pizza. British television personality Katie Hopkins also tweeted a series of rude comments about Clarkson's weight. She called Clarkson fat and asked if she ate her backup singers. For her part, Clarkson has shrugged off the comments about her weight. "I don't obsess about my weight," Clarkson said in a 2015 *Redbook* magazine interview, "which is probably one of the reasons why other people have such a problem with it."[4] In comparison, the weight of male musicians is rarely mentioned, even in passing.

SEXUALIZATION IN SONG LYRICS

While many songs have catchy beats and are fun to dance to, a closer look reveals an increasing number of songs with sexual, degrading, or misogynistic lyrics. One example of this trend is Jason Derulo's 2013 hit song "Talk Dirty." The song's lyrics include lines such as "Been around the world, don't speak the language / But your booty don't need explaining / All I really need to understand is / When you talk dirty to me."[5] These lyrics present women as objects to be used for a sexual purpose.

Songs such as Derulo's that feature sexualized lyrics are growing more common in recent years. Researchers at Brigham Young University analyzed the top 100 songs from 1959, 1969, 1979, 1989, 1999, and 2009. They looked for general and specific sexualization references. The researchers defined sexualization as when sexuality is forced on girls and their value is determined by their sexuality. The researchers discovered that sexualization in lyrics dramatically increased during the 1990s and 2000s. According to the researchers, this trend

MISOGYNY IN MUSIC

Sexism and misogyny cross all genres of music. Misogyny is a dislike of, contempt for, or a prejudice against women and girls. A misogynistic song is one that talks about women as sexual objects. It also glorifies sex without consent, or it shames women for being sexual. Song lyrics label women in demeaning terms, calling them "hoes" or "bitches." In country music, artists such as Luke Bryan and Florida Georgia Line write lyrics that reference partying and hot girls.

In hip-hop and rap, famous artists such as Eminem and Kanye West have songs that have explicit lyrics that portray women as sexual objects. Lil Wayne raps about beating up women. Rapper Rick Ross goes even further in his verse in the song "U.O.E.N.O." and promotes date rape. He raps, "Put Molly (an illegal drug) all in her champagne, she ain't even know it / I took her home and I enjoyed that, she ain't even know it."[6]

in popular music is concerning. It can influence society's values and teach young men to be sexually aggressive and treat women as objects. At the same time, they said, the sexualized lyrics also send a message to young women that their value is to provide sexual pleasure for others.

SEXISM IN MUSIC VIDEOS

In music videos, women are often sexualized and objectified. Women in the videos wear barely-there outfits. Cameras slowly pan over their bodies and exposed skin. Women dance suggestively to the music. They also look provocatively at the camera. For example, in Calvin Harris's *Summer* video, dozens of women are shown dressed in lingerie, bikinis, and cutoff shorts, often with the camera focusing on their bottoms. In contrast, Harris himself is filmed walking along a road wearing jeans and a white T-shirt. This treatment of women is not limited to a specific genre of music. It occurs in all genres, from country to rap.

In 2012, researchers at the University of Missouri studied the sexualization of women in music videos. They looked at *Billboard* Top 10 music videos over a five-year period. They found sexualization appeared in many videos, regardless of the performer's gender. They also found all genres of music showed women as sexual objects.

But the type of sexual objectification varied by genre. "While pop videos were more likely to contain sexual objectification related to movement, such as dance . . . hip hop/R&B videos were more likely to contain sexual objectification related to styling and dress,"[7] says Cynthia Frisby, an associate professor of strategic communication at the University of Missouri and one of the study's researchers. For example, women in pop videos typically dance suggestively. Women in hip hop/R&B videos will typically wear clothing that sexualizes their bodies.

"BLURRED LINES"

One of 2013's hit songs, "Blurred Lines," was also one of its most controversial. In August 2013, millions of people tuned in to the MTV Video Music Awards (VMAs). They watched Robin Thicke and Miley Cyrus perform "Blurred Lines." In the

SEX AND FEMALE ARTISTS

Male artists are not the only ones who create music videos that sexualize women. Some female musicians have created videos that portray women as objects. In Nicki Minaj's video for her hit song "Anaconda," dozens of women wiggle and gyrate in exposed skin. In the "Wrecking Ball" video, Miley Cyrus swings completely naked on a wrecking ball. And in Jennifer Lopez's collaboration with rapper Iggy Azalea, the "Booty" video features sexual images of the women rubbing their backsides together.

Some female artists say they choose to show themselves sexually onstage and in music videos because it is empowering. They are in control of their image and choose what they want to do. Superstar Beyoncé is one artist who chooses to combine conventionally sexy imagery onstage and in videos with lyrics that are anthems of female empowerment.

Critics claimed Robin Thicke's and Miley Cyrus's performance was too sexual and objectified women.

controversial performance, Cyrus wore a nude-colored bra and panties onstage. She twerked with Thicke and danced suggestively with a foam finger. The performance drew criticism and outrage from parents and fans alike.

The VMA performance was only one piece of the controversy surrounding the song. After its release earlier in 2013, the catchy tune moved up the charts as a popular party song. Some critics, however, blasted the song's lyrics, which talk about a man's belief that a girl wants to have sex but doesn't say it. Some critics argue that the song supports date rape.

The song's music video also drew criticism. The video shows three female models who wear nude-colored thongs and shoes. They dance and flirt with Thicke and his musical partners, Pharrell and T.I. All of the men are fully clothed. After public outcry, the video was banned from YouTube. However, it was still available on other Internet platforms.

The increasing sexualization of women in music videos is a concerning trend. Many people fear the sexist portrayal of women in these videos will influence the young people whose ideas about society and the role of women are being formed.

DISCUSSION STARTERS

- What differences do you notice in the way male and female musicians dress and act while performing? Why do you think these differences occur?
- Pick a current popular song. Does it have sexist lyrics? If so, what changes could you make to the lyrics to make them less sexist?
- Why do you think sexualization in music has increased in recent decades? What factors in society are driving this change?

CHAPTER FIVE

WOMEN IN
THE NEWS

The news media is a major and influential source of information for Americans. Who appears in the news and how the news media shows people and events can shape society's attitudes. The stories and people who are not covered by the news media can also have an effect. How people view gender, gender stereotypes, and sexism are reinforced by who and what they see on the news.

In the United States, six large media conglomerates control most of the news across the country: News Corp, Disney, Viacom, Time Warner, CBS, and Comcast. These large corporations control the majority of what Americans read, watch, and hear on the news. Under the control of these corporations, there are approximately 1,500 newspapers, 9,000 radio stations, 1,500 television stations, 1,000 magazines, and 2,400 publishers.[1]

FEATURED IN THE NEWS MEDIA

Many news reports feature stories about men and topics that are of interest to men. The Global Media Monitoring Project (GMMP) has been researching gender in the news media since 1995. Volunteers in 71 countries around the world tracked the presence of women in radio, television, and print news. In 1995, GMMP research found women made up only 17 percent of news subjects, defined as people who are interviewed by reporters or who are subjects of a news story.[2] Women viewers were the main consumers of news at this time. But the stories presented by media outlets were rarely about women.

However, over the past 20 years, there has been a steady increase in women featured as subjects in news stories. The latest GMMP research, conducted in 2015, found the overall presence of women featured in the news was 38 percent in print, radio, and television news combined. On the Internet and Twitter, women were featured at a slightly higher rate, at 40 percent.[3]

However, a deeper look into how men and women are featured in the news shows a few subtle differences. Women are more likely to be featured in news stories about accidents, natural disasters, and domestic violence than in stories that highlight their professional expertise

CALLED AS EXPERTS

There has been a slow increase in the number of women called upon as experts and spokespersons in news stories. In 2005, 17 percent of experts featured on the news were women. Fourteen percent of spokespersons were women. In 2015, those percentages jumped slightly to 19 percent (experts) and 20 percent (spokespersons). Typically, women appeared as government employees, public servants, activists, homemakers, and spokespersons for businesses. Even so, men still significantly outnumbered women as experts and spokespersons in 2015. Men made up 81 percent of experts and 80 percent of spokespersons in news stories.[4]

Hillary Clinton had to overcome more hurdles than many male politicians.

and abilities. Even when men and women are presented in news stories about natural disasters, poverty, or domestic violence, women are more likely than men to be shown as victims. In contrast, men are more likely to be shown as survivors. They are also more likely to be featured as both victims and survivors of war, terrorism, and state-sponsored violence. Women are more likely to be identified by their family status, such as a mother, wife, or daughter, than men are.

WOMEN IN POLITICS

In 2015, Hillary Clinton announced she was running for president of the United States in the 2016 election. The news coverage of Clinton and other women in politics often differs from how the news media covers male politicians. Women in politics are often asked about their domestic life. They are also asked how they plan to balance running for office with their roles as wives and mothers. For example, even before

SEXIST MEDIA OUTLETS

In the final days of the 2016 US presidential election, 87 percent of voters agreed they had witnessed sexism in the media's coverage of female candidates and elected officials. Name It, Change It is a nonpartisan project that studies and documents sexist media coverage of female politicians. It sponsored research asking voters to identify where they saw the most sexist treatment of female politicians in the election. Voters identified social media (27 percent), cable news (16 percent), and broadcast news (12 percent) as the biggest offenders.[5]

Clinton announced her candidacy, *USA Today* wrote in a 2014 article that it was unclear how the pregnancy of Clinton's daughter, Chelsea, would affect Clinton and her race for the presidency in 2016. In comparison, not a single news outlet asked a similar question of Mitt Romney, George W. Bush, or John McCain when each ran for president in the first decade of the 2000s.

According to a study published in 2013, the gender of a person running for office influenced newspaper articles about the candidate. In the study, researchers from Louisiana State University analyzed thousands of newspaper articles from senatorial and gubernatorial races across the United States. In each article, they looked at the candidates' genders and whether the article focused on the candidates' personality traits or political issues. They found that articles about female candidates were often more

UNBIASED LANGUAGE

In 2014, the Women's Media Center published a book, *Unspinning the Spin*, which explains how reporters, government officials, bloggers, and anyone interested in the media can use unbiased language to report the news. The purpose of the book is to foster awareness that something as simple as word choice can have a big effect on news reporting and can intentionally or unintentionally create bias and sexism. The Women's Media Center hopes the book will educate users about word choices that are accurate, inclusive, and clear and that can be used for fair and balanced reporting across all subjects.

focused on discussing character traits than articles about male candidates. When male candidates were running, news articles focused on character traits only 6 percent of the time. When only female candidates or a mix of male and female candidates were running, articles focused on character traits 9.4 and 10.8 percent of the time, respectively.[6]

Other researchers have found that the language the news media uses to describe male versus female candidates can change in meaning. For example, when the media describes a male candidate as "strong" and "assertive," these are positive qualities that demonstrate the person's strength. However, when the press uses those same words to describe a female candidate, the meaning can be negative. A 2014 report was released by the Barbara Lee Family Foundation, a nonprofit organization dedicated to promoting equality for women in politics. It stated that female politicians must demonstrate that they are both qualified and likable to win in an election. "That factor becomes a challenge in the kind of coverage that women get," says Debbie Walsh, director of the Center for American Women and Politics at Rutgers University. "If women are not portrayed as the kind of people that voters like or if the press uses certain adjectives to describe them, it calls into question whether or not they have

RAISE YOUR VOICE

When a male politician raises his voice, he is described by the media as heated, passionate, and forceful. However, when a female politician raises her voice, the media often describes her as shrill. Since Clinton entered national politics in 1992, media commentators have criticized her voice. They have described her voice as loud, shrill, grating, and harassing. Even her laugh has been labeled a "cackle."[8] Journalists describe her speeches as shouting, shrieking, and screaming. Using these words to describe Clinton's speaking style diminishes her likability and credibility because of her gender, not because of the content in her speeches.

Clinton is not the only female politician to be criticized in the media for her speaking style. Former British prime minister Margaret Thatcher was also criticized for being too shrill. Thatcher even received vocal training to modify the tone, pitch, and tempo of her voice. Conversely, German leader Angela Merkel has been criticized in the media for her monotone speaking style.

the credentials they need to succeed."[7]

FOCUS ON APPEARANCE

For many women in the news, coverage about their appearance and clothing choices is common. In 2009, news commentator Matt Drudge commented on a female senator's appearance, calling her fat. Stories in the *New York Times* and *Washington Post* have focused on a female senator's purses and a White House counsel's shoe collection. Entire articles have been written about Clinton's hair and former Speaker of the House Nancy Pelosi's clothing. At the same time, there are very few, if any, articles that feature details about a male senator's tie collection, choice of suits, or hairstyles.

Age is another area in which the news media treats men and

Nancy Pelosi serves California's 12th district in the House of Representatives.

women differently. Prior to the 2016 presidential election, several articles questioned whether Clinton was too old to run for president. However, several previous male candidates, including Ronald Reagan and Bob Dole, were the same age or older than Clinton. Even the eventual winner of the 2016 presidential election, Donald Trump, was older than Clinton.

According to some research, all of this attention paid to a female politician's appearance may have a negative effect on her campaign. A study was released in 2013 by the Women's Media Center. It found that a woman's appearance when she was running for political office had a negative impact on her electability. This proved to be true whether the mentions in the media were flattering, unflattering, or neutral. In the research, there was no impact on electability of male politicians when study participants read similar comments about their appearance.

Celinda Lake of Lake Research Partners says that even minor sexism in the media can damage a female candidate on Election Day. She says that someone in the media writing that a candidate is an "ice queen" or a "mean girl" can be just as damaging as using overt sexist language. Lake also believes this type of sexist treatment in the media may stop some women from running for office.

"And there's no question that all this deters women from getting into politics. If someone who is a treasurer and a lieutenant governor of a state can be called an 'ice queen,' if someone [who] is a sitting U.S. senator can be called 'a mean girl,' then, gosh, women think, 'Why am I going to try this? I'm not,'" says Lake.[9]

Both Lake and Walsh believe women need to take control of how they are shown by the media. Women also need to speak out when they see sexist language and treatment. "As women, we all have a role in calling this out," says Lake. "But young women, in particular, can make this difference. On social media and on all these platforms, they can call it out and pass it on. They can make this a movement and demand change."[10]

DISCUSSION STARTERS

- Examine the front page of a local newspaper or online news source. How many articles feature women? Is there a difference in the articles about women versus those focused on men?
- What examples have you seen of words that are gender biased in news coverage? How could you replace them with gender-neutral words?
- How does news coverage influence gender stereotypes?

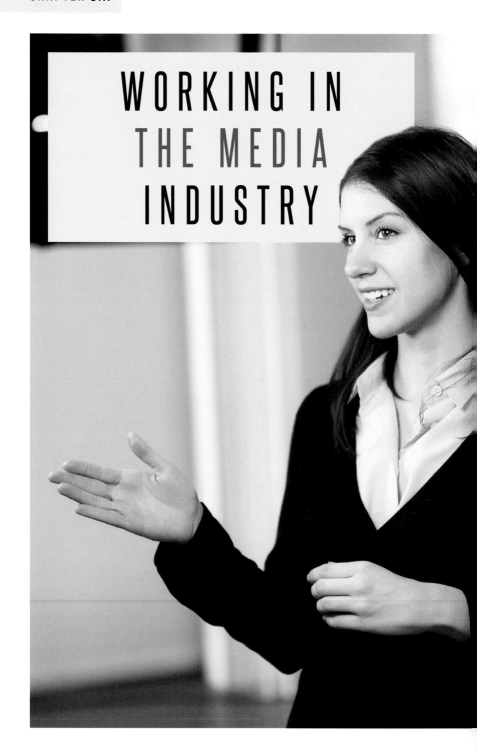

CHAPTER SIX

WORKING IN THE MEDIA INDUSTRY

Across all media platforms, women work in a variety of careers. Some women work in front of the cameras as reporters and news anchors. Others work behind the scenes as editors, producers, directors, and more. Yet they are still underrepresented throughout the media's workforce. This disparity can affect the choices regarding which news stories are run, which types of films and television shows are made, and how various subjects are handled in the media.

WORKING IN THE NEWS MEDIA

The people who report the news are just as important as what the news story is. Often, the reporter determines which stories to feature and how to portray the people involved in a story. Therefore, having a balanced and diverse newsroom can lead to more balanced and inclusionary news stories in the media.

According to a 2015 study by the Women's Media Center, women working in the news media are assigned to report stories at a substantially lower rate than their male colleagues. In the nightly broadcast news, female reporters are on camera 32 percent of the time. In print news, women report 37 percent of the stories. On the Internet, women write 42 percent of the stories, while on the news wires, which are electronically transmitted up-to-the-minute news services, women are assigned only 38 percent of the stories.[1] "Our research shows that media needs to do better," says Julie Burton, president of the Women's Media Center. "The bottom line is this: Overwhelmingly, men still dominate media. Women are 51 percent of the population—but hardly equal partners in telling the story. Society is best served when the media accurately reflect the population."[2]

IN THE NEWSROOM

At traditional newspapers, women staffers remain in the minority. According to the American Society of News Editors (ASNE), women made up approximately 38 percent of daily-newspaper employees in 2016. For online news organizations, the percentage was higher, with women making up nearly 50 percent of employees.[3]

DIGITAL NEWSROOMS

Some good news regarding men and women in the media can be found in digital newsrooms. Compared with many traditional print or television newsrooms, digital newsrooms have less of a traditional hierarchy that uses several layers of supervisors and managers. Instead, digital newsrooms have a more flat organizational structure, with few or no levels of middle management between staff and executives. According to Cory Haik, the executive producer and senior editor for digital news at the *Washington Post*, employees with the necessary skills, whether they are men or women, are going to be put in charge of leading a team. Writer Anna Griffin says millennials, who frequently staff digital newsrooms, have a different set of expectations than older news employees. They realize the need for diverse voices and have fewer biases and preconceptions about what a leader should look like. When they think about an editor, they are just as likely to think of a woman as a man.

"We must ask ourselves how we can do a better job of inspiring people of color and women to go into the profession, hire them at good wages, and give them opportunities to influence coverage and advance through the ranks," says ASNE president Pam Fine.[4]

In television news, women have made some gains in the newsroom. According to the Radio Television Digital News Association/Hofstra University Annual Survey, the numbers of female television news directors and news staffers in 2015 rose to their highest levels since 1995. But across all television newsrooms surveyed, only 33 percent of news directors were women, while 44 percent of all staffers were female. In radio, the numbers are lower, with women working as 24 percent of news directors and 32 percent of general staffers.[5]

DRIVERS OF THE MEDIA'S GENDER GAP

According to Nieman Reports, women attend communications schools and enter journalism in approximately the same numbers as men. However, women leave the field in greater numbers. By the time journalists reach 20 years of experience, only one-third of them are women.[6]

Some people believe the gender imbalance in journalism occurs because of professional and social factors that favor men. Journalism careers often have intense and irregular hours. Reporters are required to cover stories and interview subjects at all hours of the day and night. They are also expected to travel for hours to cover a story at a moment's notice. In many families, women do most of the work raising children and keeping the home. These responsibilities can be extremely difficult to balance with the demands of a career in journalism.

Another factor may be the type of news that male and female journalists report. Men typically cover hard news topics such as politics and world news. Women are more likely to report softer news topics such as fashion, entertainment, and dining. An analysis of thousands of

The Independent Association of Publishers' Employees 1096 union found that male journalists earn slightly more than females with twice as much experience.

New York Times articles in 2014 showed that women wrote the majority of the stories in the fashion, dining, home, travel, and health sections. In contrast, men wrote the majority of the stories in the seven largest sections,

including US news, world news, opinion, and business. Because many organizations turn to journalists working in hard news to promote into management positions, women are being left out of the discussion.

Another factor that may discourage women from pursuing jobs in the newsroom is the difference between their pay and the pay of their male colleagues. The Independent Association of Publishers' Employees 1096 is the union that represents journalists at several publications owned by Dow Jones. In 2016, it reported that the news corporation paid its male employees more than it did women, even if they had similar levels of experience. For example, male employees with up to five years of experience earned an average of 13.5 percent more than female employees with the same experience. The union found that on average, women working full-time in nonsupervisory positions at Dow Jones–owned companies earned approximately 87 cents for every dollar earned by men working full-time.[7]

In some cases, differences in pay are justified. A specific reporter or editor could have special skills he or she brings to the job. Or the job market could have influenced an employee's pay at the time of his or her hiring. However, these variations are unlikely to explain the overall gap between men and women working in news. Instead, the pay gap may be linked to the lack of women in top newsroom jobs to make hiring, promotion, and assignment decisions. According to the ASNE's 2016 survey, men dominate supervisory roles in newsrooms, while only 37 percent of supervisors are women.[8] "It's really important to take a look structurally at the news business and ask: Why, when you look at the highest levels, are women not there?" says Elisa Lees Muñoz, executive director of the International Women's Media Foundation, a Washington-based group that supports women in journalism.[9]

These factors can create a continuing cycle. Men in leadership positions are more likely to promote other men to management. As women see fewer females occupying these top roles and fewer opportunities available for them, they become more likely to leave the industry. This leaves fewer women with the necessary experience to apply for management roles, which makes men in the business even more likely to advance into top positions.

THE RISE OF WOMEN IN 2016

During the 2016 presidential election cycle, several women rose to top positions on air and behind the scenes across the major news networks. Women such as Dana Bash at CNN, Kristen Welker at NBC, Nancy Cordes at CBS News, Jennifer Griffin at Fox News, and Cecilia Vega at ABC News were an integral part of election media coverage. On cable, MSNBC host Rachel Maddow experienced an election-related ratings surge as she became a critical voice speaking against Trump's candidacy. Industry experts say because the Republican race was so wide open and included a large number of candidates, it created more opportunities for experienced political reporters, many of whom were women.

DOUBLE STANDARD FOR LEADERSHIP

Some people claim there is a double standard for male and female leaders in journalism. As in the political sphere, qualities that are praised in men are sometimes criticized in women. In 2014, *New York Times* executive editor Jill Abramson was let go by the paper. Anonymous sources claim that Abramson's demeanor was a factor in her firing and that she lost the support of her newsroom by being uncaring and brusque. "I was a hard-charging editor, and there were some people who worked for me that didn't like that style," says Abramson. "Women in leadership roles are scrutinized constantly and sometimes differently than men."[10]

According to Janet Coats, the former executive editor at the *Sarasota Herald-Tribune*, women in the media are faced with an unwinnable double standard. They are expected to be tough, strong, and assertive in order to be considered for management positions. At the same time, once they are hired into management, many expect them to be more nurturing and caring than their male colleagues.

FILM AND TELEVISION ENTERTAINMENT

In 2016, women made up only 17 percent of all directors, writers, producers, executive producers, editors, and cinematographers in the 250 top-grossing domestic films, according to a study sponsored by the Center for the Study of Women in Television and Film at San Diego State University. This number showed a decline of two percentage points from 2015 and was the same percentage as in 1998. In 2016, only 7 percent of these films had a

Many more men than women work behind the scenes in the entertainment industry.

On average, male directors have longer careers in Hollywood than female directors do.

female director, a decrease of two percentage points from 2015 and 1998.[11]

These numbers highlight the fact that the opportunities for women working behind the camera in Hollywood have changed little in almost 20 years. Instead, men, and in particular white men, continue to hold the power in Hollywood. "They make decisions about what gets made and doesn't get made. They tend to make things that resonate with their experiences and their tastes, and the appreciation of men they socialize with," says Darnell Hunt, director of the University of California, Los Angeles's Ralph J. Bunche Center for African American Studies.[12]

In television, women did not fare much better. During the 2014–2015 network television season, women directed only 16 percent of episodes that aired on network and cable television channels, according to an annual analysis by the Directors Guild of America (DGA). This percentage was a small increase of two percentage points from 2013. "The uptick in the number of episodes directed by women—modest but hopeful—is just a drop in the bucket of what needs to be done . . . before we can begin to realize equal opportunities in television for our members," said DGA president Paris Barclay.[13]

DISCUSSION STARTERS

- How can hiring and promoting more women reduce sexism in the media?
- What factors act as barriers to women working in journalism and taking on leadership roles in media organizations? What can people do to break down these barriers?
- Why do you think there are fewer opportunities for women behind the camera in newsrooms? How can this be changed?

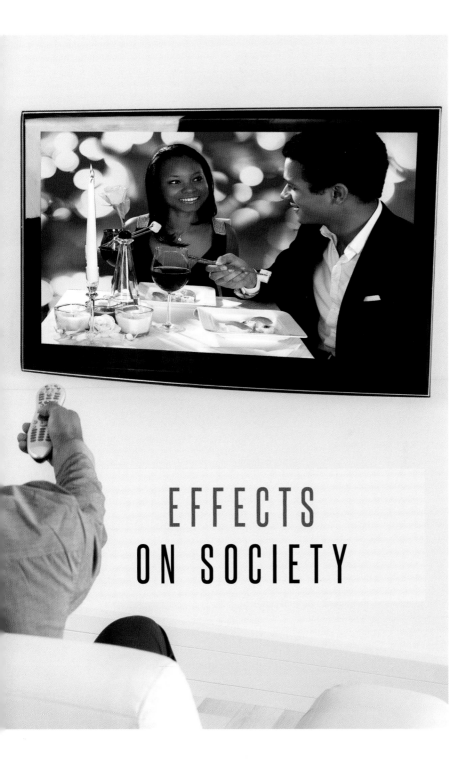

CHAPTER SEVEN

EFFECTS
ON SOCIETY

According to Nielsen's Q1 2016 Total Audience report, Americans spent more than ten hours per day consuming media in the first quarter of 2016, a full hour more than the same quarter in 2015.[1] The media consumption was spread across several platforms including live television, radio, print, and digital devices. Smartphone and tablet use soared, jumping 37 and 12 minutes, respectively.[2] "I think the sheer volume of media technology that kids are exposed to on a daily basis is mind-boggling," says James Steyer, CEO and founder of Common Sense Media.

TEENS AND MEDIA

According to a 2015 study by Common Sense Media, a nonprofit that helps families manage media and technology, American teens spend nine hours each day watching television, videos, and movies, playing video games, reading online articles, listening to music, and reading social media.[4] That is more than the average teen spends sleeping or in school each day. Tweens aged 8 to 12 were not much better, spending about six hours per day consuming media.[5]

"It just shows you that these kids live in this massive 24/7 digital media technology world, and it's shaping every aspect of their life. They spend far more time with media technology than any other thing in their life."[3]

Because media in various forms are such a large part of life, the images presented by the media can have an enormous effect on the way people see themselves and the world around them. Specifically, media's representation of women and girls can have a huge impact on how society views women, as well as on public attitudes toward women and gender equality.

UNREALISTIC EXPECTATIONS AFFECT BODY IMAGE

Manipulated images across media platforms create unrealistic expectations for teens and others in society. The edited images of beauty and perfection presented by the media do not reflect what models look like in real life. But they send a message to girls and women that they need to be young, thin, and beautiful. In addition, the media's photo manipulation reduces the number of body shapes and sizes in the media. This pushes society's definition of beauty toward a single standard.

Being bombarded by unrealistic images of female bodies and beauty can have several negative effects on teens and young adults. Constantly comparing oneself with the unrealistic beauty standards pushed by the media can damage a teen's self-image and

MORE EDUCATION NEEDED

Even though many people know the media digitally manipulates images, they are still affected by what they see. Therefore, more education is needed to empower people to challenge these representations of women in the media and stand up for more realistic representations across all media platforms. Because children's exposure to media messaging begins at such a young age, the earlier media-literacy education begins, the better prepared children and young adults will be.

self-esteem. According to a Girl Scouts Research Institute survey, nearly one-half of girls aged 13 to 17 responded that they wished they were as skinny as the models in fashion magazines. Almost 50 percent also responded that the models in fashion magazines gave them a body image to strive for. In another survey by the *Today* show and AOL.com, approximately 80 percent of teen girls said they compared themselves with media images of celebrities, and nearly half of them said the comparison made them feel dissatisfied with the way they look.[6]

In some cases, constantly comparing themselves to images in the media can cause girls and women to develop extremely negative body images. When this occurs, they may become fixated on the parts of their bodies they dislike. This fixation can lead to several damaging psychiatric conditions such as depression, obsessive-compulsive disorders, and body dysmorphic disorder. These disorders can disrupt a person's health and quality of life.

Poor body image can also cause some girls and women to develop unhealthy eating habits to try to make themselves look like the images they see in the media. According to the National Eating Disorders Association, more than 50 percent of teenage girls in the United States use unhealthy weight control behaviors such as skipping meals, smoking cigarettes, vomiting, and taking laxatives. Over time, these unhealthy weight control behaviors can develop into anorexia, bulimia, and other serious eating disorders. In the United States, 20 million women suffer from an eating disorder.[7] These disorders can have serious health consequences, including abnormally slow heart rate and low blood pressure, an increased risk of heart failure, a reduction in bone density, severe dehydration (which can lead to kidney failure), and muscle loss and weakness. In some severe cases, eating disorders can also lead to death.

SEXUAL EXPLOITATION

In sexualized ads, women often appear ready to do a man's bidding. This portrayal sends a message to audiences that these qualities are normal and desirable in women. It can also harm a young girl's self-image, her emotional development, and her expectations of relationships.

In 2007, the American Psychological Association (APA)

RETOUCHING PHOTOS

Digital photo retouching has become so common that many people are doing it before they post a picture on social media. According to a 2014 survey conducted by Harris Interactive, 70 percent of Generation Y/ millennial women edit their pictures before posting on social media.[8] They remove blemishes, add color, and make themselves look thinner. Body image expert Adrienne Ressler says she is concerned that so much self-editing of photos can fuel negative self-esteem and body image issues, putting a person at risk for future problems with eating disorders and other destructive behaviors.

The sexualized images of girls and young women found throughout the media can have harmful effects on women and society.

released a report on the effects of sexualized images of girls and young women in advertising, merchandising, and media. Researchers studied the content of almost all types of media, including television, music videos, music lyrics, magazines, movies, video games, and the Internet. They also studied advertising campaigns and products that targeted girls. In the study, researchers found the large number of sexualized images of girls in the media was harmful to girls' self-image and development.

The study found that exposure to sexualized images and lyrics caused girls to be less confident in their own bodies, which led to emotional problems, such as shame and anxiety. Sexualization in the media was also linked to three common mental health problems: eating disorders, depression, and low self-esteem. The study also found evidence that sexualization of girls in the media had a negative effect on young women's ability to develop a healthy sexual self-image.

In order to combat the negative effects of the images that surround young people in the media, all students should be taught how to recognize sexualization in the media and understand the effects it can have on society. "As a society, we need to replace all of these sexualized images with ones showing girls in positive settings—ones that show the uniqueness and competence of girls," says Eileen L. Zurbriggen, an associate professor of psychology at the University of California, Santa Cruz.[9]

DISCUSSION STARTERS

- What forms of media do you use daily? How many hours do you spend consuming media each day? How does that compare with the national averages?
- Why do you believe the media sexualize young women and girls?
- Compare the effects of the media on both male and female body images. Do you think boys and men can also suffer from negative body image issues caused by the media?

CHAPTER EIGHT

WORKING FOR CHANGE IN THE MEDIA

Sexism exists in many forms throughout the media. It can be found in the sexualized and digitally altered images of women used in advertising, the stereotyped portrayals of female characters in film and television, and the way the media cover women's stories in the news and in sports. Sexism exists in the workplace at newspaper offices, television news networks, and other media industry companies, affecting women's opportunities for assignments and advancement.

Many people are working to change the way media represent women. They are identifying examples of sexism in the media and calling out the media platforms and organizations responsible. They hope their efforts to increase public awareness about the issue and its serious consequences will help reduce or eliminate sexism in the media.

THE ROLE OF SOCIAL MEDIA

As recently as the early 2000s, it was difficult to fight sexism in the media publicly. Letter-writing campaigns were only seen by a few people. Rallies and other anti-sexism events could gather larger crowds, but people were often only able to participate if they lived near the cities where these events took place. There were few places where people could easily discuss the issues with a broader public audience.

The arrival of social media has significantly opened up the doors of protest to people all over the country and the world, regardless of where they live. Social media sites such as Facebook, Twitter, Tumblr, and Instagram have made activism against sexism easier than ever. Through these sites, people around the world can create public dialogues about sexism.

In 2013, women turned to social media to protest a T-shirt sold by the Children's Place clothing company. The T-shirt for girls showed a checklist of "my best subjects" with shopping, music, and dancing all checked. Math was not checked and had the words "well, nobody's perfect" written underneath it.[1] Customers flooded the company's Facebook page with complaints about the shirt, calling it insensitive and

NAME IT, CHANGE IT

In 2010, the Women's Media Center, the Women's Campaign Forum Foundation, and Political Parity joined together to launch the Name It, Change It project. This national campaign works to end widespread sexist coverage of women. It particularly focuses on female political candidates and all members of the press, including bloggers, radio hosts, and television reporters. The campaign identifies sexist treatment of women in the media and coordinates national efforts to respond to these incidents. The campaign monitors and holds media outlets accountable for sexist coverage, sending thousands of letters and e-mails to offenders. It also works proactively with media professionals and outlets to help them provide fair and balanced coverage of elections.

#NOTBUYINGIT

During the Super Bowl, the television commercials are almost as anticipated as the game on the field. Every year, advertisers use stereotypes and sex to sell everything from cars to Internet service. Now, social media users are using a Twitter hashtag, #NotBuyingIt, to call out sexist ads and express their disgust as they watch the game in real time. In 2013, one of the ads that drew the most criticism was for web host GoDaddy.com. The commercial featured a long, deep kiss between a supermodel and a nerdy computer programmer. The ad drew criticism on Twitter, with many people tweeting that it stereotyped computer programmers and objectified women. During the 2013 Super Bowl, the #NotBuyingIt hashtag generated more than 10,000 tweets and reached more than eight million people during the game.[3]

sexist. The company responded to the public pressure and pulled the shirt from stores and issued an apology to customers on its Facebook page. "We take feedback from our customers very seriously," the company's Facebook post explained. "It has come to our attention that some of you view our Best Subjects T shirt as insensitive towards girls and women. This was not our intent. There are countless women in all walks of life who excel in math, including our very own CEO. We have pulled this product from our stores and we want to express our apologies to anyone we may have offended."[2]

On Twitter, the #AskHerMore campaign is inspiring people to call out sexist reporting and refocus the media on highlighting women's achievements instead of their appearance. Launched in 2014 by filmmaker Jennifer Siebel Newsom, the campaign encourages reporters to ask women substantive questions instead of questions about their fashion and diet. Twitter users can use the #AskHerMore hashtag to tweet out questions they want reporters to ask, such as what an actress learned from a character she portrayed or what an actress still wants to accomplish in her career.

At the 2017 Golden Globe Awards, more than eight million people tweeted using the hashtag. They called on reporters to ask actresses on the red carpet about more

Social media can be a powerful tool when used to create social change.

than their appearance and what designer dress they were wearing. Award-winning actress Reese Witherspoon talked to ABC News interviewer Robin Roberts on the 2015 Academy Awards red carpet about her support for the Twitter campaign. "This is a movement to say we're more than just our dresses. There are 44 nominees this year that are women and we are so happy to be here and talk about the work that we've done," said Witherspoon.[4]

Bowing to public pressure from everyday people on social media, some companies are making changes. In 2014, Victoria's Secret launched an ad that displayed the words "Perfect Body" across an image of ten extremely thin models wearing the company's lingerie.[5] Thousands of people protested the ad on Twitter and in a Change. org petition, saying it promoted unhealthy and unrealistic body images. The company responded and removed the advertising slogan, replacing it with "A Body for Every Body."[6] And in 2017, more commercials shown during the Super Bowl were filled with heartwarming messages, including commercials that celebrated diversity. "This dramatic shift didn't happen on its own—consumers have made their voices heard at the Super Bowl and throughout the past four years with our #NotBuyingIt campaign," says Newsom, who is also the founder of the Representation Project, an organization that works to create a world

Some companies are using more diverse models to sell their products.

free from stereotypes and social injustice. "As a result, advertisers, media outlets, and brands are listening, ensuring a Super Bowl full of inclusive ads that uplift our culture, rather than demean it."[7]

Although social media will not replace traditional activism such as peaceful protests, demonstrations, and rallies, it can give a voice to people who have been unable to participate and speak out about sexism in the media. No matter where they are located or the resources they have, their voices can be heard.

A CAMPAIGN TO END SEXISM IN THE NEWS MEDIA

Recognizing that sexism in the media is a global problem, several organizations have joined together to fight sexism in world journalism. In 2016, the World Association for Christian Communication (WACC), the GMMP, and other partners announced the launch of an advocacy campaign with the goal of ending news media sexism. The campaign aims to support and highlight efforts in countries around the world to end sexism in the media. Members of the campaign hope these efforts will help develop effective strategies to create fair and equal representation of men and women in the media. "This is a call for action to all those who are committed to gender equality. Media have a significant impact on how we perceive our reality," says Dr. Karin Achtelstetter, general secretary of WACC.

USING YOUTUBE FOR CHANGE

Actress Geena Davis has partnered with three successful female creators from YouTube for #ShesGotDrive, a new campaign for gender equality in media. Lifestyle personality Taryn Southern, musician Clara C., and filmmaker Yulin Kuang are joining Davis in the campaign to promote gender equality throughout the media and entertainment industries. The YouTube women are creating content that highlights their path to success in the entertainment industry through YouTube. By sharing how they navigated their careers in male-dominated industries, they hope to inspire other young women.

"The campaign will tackle these issues and challenge media outlets to take professional ethics for gender-fair practice seriously."[8]

SIGNS OF CHANGE

Although there are still rampant examples of sexism in the media, there have also been signs of positive change. In the entertainment industry, roles for women on television and in films have become more varied and complex in recent years. In 2016, the number of female protagonists in movies increased by seven percentage points.[9] And for only the third time in history, three films with a female lead or co-lead were nominated for Best Picture at the 2017 Academy Awards: *Hidden Figures*, *Arrival*, and *La La Land*. These films showcased complex female characters, allowing the actors to show more than their sex appeal on-screen. The National Aeronautics and Space Administration (NASA) mathematicians of *Hidden Figures*, the linguistics scientist in *Arrival*, and the hardworking actress in *La La Land* represent the type of characters that men traditionally play in Oscar-nominated movies. These characters are defined by their work and not their personal relationships. *Hidden*

THIS GIRL CAN

Rather than making women and girls feel bad about their bodies, organizations such as Sport England are using the media to encourage women of all shapes and sizes to take pride in their bodies and motivate them to exercise. The This Girl Can campaign seeks to tell the real story of women who play sports by using images of real women who sweat and jiggle rather than the edited and styled images typically found in the media.

Octavia Spencer, Taraji P. Henson, and Janelle Monáe starred in *Hidden Figures.*

Figures in particular is the first Best Picture nominee to feature a cast of highly educated African-American female characters pursuing a heroic, professional goal.

Advertisers are also beginning to think more about how they feature women in ads. In 2016, Unilever, the corporation behind more than 400 brands including Ben & Jerry's ice cream and Dove soap, pledged to remove sexist stereotypes from its ads. The second-biggest advertiser in the world, Unilever also called on its competitors to do the same. Chief marketing officer Keith Weed said the company's large global reach gives it a responsibility to push change throughout the world.

He said Unilever's campaign to end gender stereotypes in its ads, called Unstereotype, was the product of two years of research on the issue. Unilever found that one-half of its ads stereotyped both men and women. "If we looked at role, personality and appearance, then they weren't representing women as they are today. Some of the imagery might have been current years ago, but it certainly wasn't today," says Weed.[10] Now, the company plans to create ads that more realistically and fairly portray women.

Although there has been some progress in reducing sexism in the media, there is still a lot more work to be done. By understanding the subtle ways sexism can appear throughout the media and the effect it can have on audiences worldwide, people can make changes to bring about more equal and inclusive media for all people, regardless of gender.

DISCUSSION STARTERS

- How can the average person help reduce sexism in the media?
- What signs of improvement and gender equality have you noticed in your local media?
- How has social media helped people work for change in the media?

ESSENTIAL FACTS

SIGNIFICANT EVENTS

- Woodbury Soap Company was the first to advertise its product using sexual content. In 1911, the company released an ad that implied women who used the soap would have "Skin You Love to Touch."

- In 2004, beauty brand Dove introduced its Campaign for Real Beauty. The advertising campaign featured women of all shapes, sizes, and ages who looked beautiful without having their bodies digitally altered.

- The arrival of social media in the 2000s significantly opened up the doors of protest to women all over the country and the world, regardless of where they live. With a few keystrokes, protesters can interact with a worldwide audience and promote awareness and change.

KEY PLAYERS

- Madonna Badger is the founder of advertising agency Badger & Winters. She has pledged to create ads that do not objectify women and is encouraging other advertising professionals to do the same.

- Hollywood film producer Ross Putman has worked to highlight sexism in Hollywood scripts by creating a Twitter account where he tweets the first description of a female character in an unproduced script. Putman's account has gained nearly 60,000 followers.

- Actress Reese Witherspoon founded her own production company, Pacific Standard, after becoming fed up with being offered below-standard acting roles. Pacific Standard has had success with its films *Gone Girl* and *Wild*, which have earned its leading actresses nominations for best actress at the Academy Awards and Golden Globe Awards.

IMPACT ON SOCIETY

For decades, sexism in the media has affected women of all ages, races, professions, and nationalities. In the media, sexism can occur in many forms, such as the images used in advertising, the portrayal of female characters in film, and the coverage of women in the media. Sexism also affects women working in the media industry. It affects their opportunities for story assignments and advancement. In recent years, many people have begun to stand up and speak out against this unfair treatment of women in the media. By recognizing the small ways sexism is apparent in the media and its effects on both women and men, viewers can work to change how women are represented in all forms of media.

QUOTE

"Agencies create advertising that promotes not only the product, but also the people who make it. Ads should never 'use people' or take advantage of women and men in any way, shape or form."

—Madonna Badger, the founder of advertising agency Badger & Winters

GLOSSARY

ACTIVISM

The policy or action of using vigorous campaigning to bring about political or social change.

ANOREXIA

An emotional disorder characterized by an obsessive desire to lose weight by refusing to eat.

BULIMIA

An eating disorder in which a large quantity of food is consumed in a short period of time, followed by forced vomiting and feelings of guilt or shame.

DISMEMBERMENT AD

An ad that features pieces of a person's body as disconnected objects.

HYPERSEXUALIZATION

Depicting or treating woman as sexual objects, or using marketing or products to encourage girls to act in sexual ways.

MISOGYNY

An attitude that looks down on women and girls.

PORTRAY

To describe or present someone or something in a particular way.

PROVOCATIVELY

In a manner intended to arouse sexual desire or interest.

SEXUALIZATION

Attributing a sexual role to a woman.

STEREOTYPE

A widely held but oversimplified idea about a particular type of person or thing.

SUBMISSIVE

Willing to yield or give in to others.

ADDITIONAL RESOURCES

SELECTED BIBLIOGRAPHY

Griffin, Anna. "Where Are the Women?" *Nieman Reports*. President and Fellows of Harvard College, September 11, 2014. Web. 21 June 2017.

Lauzen, Martha M. "The Celluloid Ceiling: Behind-the-Scenes Employment of Women on the Top 100, 250, and 500 Films of 2016." *The Center for the Study of Women in Television and Film*. Dr. Martha Lauzen, 2017. Web. 21 June 2017.

Rogers, Katie. "Sure, These Women Are Winning Olympic Medals, but Are They Single?" *New York Times*. New York Times, Aug. 18, 2016. Web. 21 June 2017.

FURTHER READINGS

Barcella, Laura. *Fight Like a Girl: 50 Feminists Who Changed the World*. San Francisco, CA: Zest, 2016. Print.

Bates, Laura. *Everyday Sexism*. New York: Thomas Dunne, 2016. Print.

Marciniak, Kristin. *Women in Arts and Entertainment*. Minneapolis, MN: Abdo, 2016. Print.

ONLINE RESOURCES

To learn more about sexism in the media, visit **abdobooklinks.com**. These links are routinely monitored and updated to provide the most current information available.

MORE INFORMATION

For more information on this subject, contact or visit the following organizations:

ALLIANCE FOR WOMEN IN MEDIA
2365 Harrodsburg Road, A325
Lexington, KY 40504
202-750-3664
allwomeninmedia.org

The Alliance for Women in Media is an organization dedicated to supporting women across all media segments.

CENTER FOR THE STUDY OF WOMEN IN TELEVISION AND FILM
San Diego State University
5500 Campanile Drive
San Diego, CA 92182
619-594-6301
womenintvfilm.sdsu.edu

The Center for the Study of Women in Television and Film generates a number of large annual studies on women's representation and portrayals in film and television.

SOURCE NOTES

CHAPTER 1. SEXISM AT THE SUMMER OLYMPICS

1. Madison Park. "Is Olympic Coverage Undercutting Women's Achievements?" *CNN*. Cable News Network, 9 Aug. 2016. Web. 2 Aug. 2017.

2. Ibid.

3. Katie Rogers. "Sure, These Women Are Winning Olympic Medals, but Are They Single?" *New York Times*. New York Times, 18 Aug. 2016. Web. 2 Aug. 2017.

4. Karen Given. "Corey Cogdell-Unrein on Being in the Eye of a Twitterstorm," *WBUR*. WBUR, 12 Aug. 2016. Web. 2 Aug. 2017.

5. Kayla Lombardo. "Corey-Cogdell-Unrein: Women Should Be Recognized Outside of Who We're Married To." *Excellesports*. Excelle Sports, 9 Aug. 2016. Web. 2 Aug. 2017.

6. Aaron Hutchins. "Why Men Shouldn't Get the Credit When Women Win in Rio." *Maclean's*. Rogers Media, 9 Aug. 2016. Web. 2 Aug. 2017.

7. Martha Tesema. "Chicago Tribune Scrutinized for Sexist Olympic Medalist Headline." *Mashable*. Mashable, 8 Aug. 2016. Web. 2 Aug. 2017.

8. David Bauder. "NBC Swim Commentator Defends Comments Criticized as Sexist." *AP News*. Associated Press, 7 Aug. 2016. Web. 2 Aug. 2017.

9. Christina Cauterucci. "Olympics Sexism Watch: Wives, Broadcast Delays, and Swimming 'Like a Man.'" *Slate*. The State Group, 8 Aug. 2016. Web. 3 Aug. 2017.

10. "Rio 2018: #Covertheathlete Hashtag Takes Aim at Sexist Coverage of Female Athletes." *ABC*. ABC, 17 Aug. 2016. Web. 2 Aug. 2017.

11. Katie Rogers. "Sure, These Women Are Winning Olympic Medals, but Are They Single?" *New York Times*. New York Times, 18 Aug. 2016. Web. 2 Aug. 2017.

12. Kiley Kroh. "SportsCenter's Shameful Coverage of Women's Sports." *ThinkProgress*. Think Progress, 12 June 2015. Web. 2 Aug. 2017.

13. Ibid.

14. "Delle Donne Named 2015 WNBA MVP." *NBA*. NBA Media Ventures, 16 Sept. 2015. Web. 3 Aug. 2017.

CHAPTER 2. SEXISM IN ADVERTISING

1. Lara O'Reilly. "Lingerie Company CEO Demands Calvin Klein Rips Down Its 'Sexist' Fetty Wap and Klara Kristin Billboard." *Business Insider*. Business Insider, 18 Mar. 2016. Web. 2 Aug. 2017.

2. Ibid.

3. Ibid.

4. "History of Advertising No 87: The First Ad with Sex Appeal." *Campaign*. Haymarket Media Group, 16 Jan. 2014. Web. 3 Aug. 2017.

5. Deanna Michalopoulos. "Why Is Objectification Bad? The Sneaky Way Women's Bodies Are Cropped to Pieces." *Bustle*. BGD, 29 Apr. 2014. Web. 2 Aug. 2017.

6. Emanuella Grinberg. "How to Create Ads That Don't Objectify Women." *CNN*. Cable News Network, 18 Feb. 2016. Web. 2 Aug. 2017.

7. Ibid.

8. Ibid.

CHAPTER 3. PORTRAYAL OF WOMEN ON-SCREEN

1. Brent Lang. "Number of Female Film Protagonists Hits High in 2016 (Study)." *Variety.* Variety Media, 21 Feb. 2017. Web. 3 Aug. 2017.

2. Dr. Martha M. Lauzen. "It's a Man's (Celluloid) World: Portrayals of Female Characters in the Top 100 Films of 2016." *Center for the Study of Women in Television & Film.* Dr. Martha Lauzen, n.d. Web. 3 Aug. 2017.

3. Rosie Fletcher. "Leading Roles for Women in Hollywood Reach an All-Time High . . . Which Is Still Pathetically Low." *Digital Spy.* Hearst Magazines UK, 22 Feb. 2017. Web. 3 Aug. 2017.

4. Dr. Martha M. Lauzen. "It's a Man's (Celluloid) World: Portrayals of Female Characters in the Top 100 Films of 2016." *Center for the Study of Women in Television & Film.* Dr. Martha Lauzen, n.d. Web. 3 Aug. 2017.

5. Ibid.

6. Dr. Martha M. Lauzen. "Boxed in 2015–16: Women On Screen and Behind the Scenes in Television." *Center for the Study of Women in Television & Film.* Dr. Martha Lauzen, Sept. 2016. Web. 3 Aug. 2017.

7. Brent Lang. "Number of Female Film Protagonists Hits High in 2016 (Study)." *Variety.* Variety Media, 21 Feb. 2017. Web. 3 Aug. 2017.

8. USC Annenberg Staff. "Gender Stereotypes Persist in Films on a Worldwide Scale." *USC News.* University of Southern California, 22 Sept. 2014. Web. 3 Aug. 2017.

9. Ibid.

10. Public Affairs Staff. "Screening Sexy: Film Females and the Story That Isn't Changing." *USC Annenberg.* University of Southern California, 13 May 2013. Web. 3 Aug. 2017.

11. Eliana Dockterman. "Read All the Sexist Ways Female Characters Are Introduced in Scripts." *Time.* Time, 10 Feb. 2016. Web. 3 Aug. 2017.

12. Samantha Ellis. "Why the Bechdel Test Doesn't (Always) Work." *Guardian.* Guardian News and Media Limited, 20 Aug. 2016. Web. 3 Aug. 2017.

13. Ben Child, "Reese Witherspoon Blows Whistle on Hollywood Sexism: 'I Don't Want to Be the Girlfriend in a Dumb Comedy" *Guardian.* Guardian News and Media Limited, 4 Feb. 2016. Web. 3 Aug. 2017.

CHAPTER 4. SEXISM AND THE MUSIC INDUSTRY

1. Guardian Staff. "Bjork on Sexism: 'Women in Music Are Allowed to Sing about Their Boyfriends.'" *Guardian.* Guardian News and Media Limited, 21 Dec. 2016. Web. 3 Aug. 2017.

2. Ibid.

3. Marissa R. Moss. "We Need to Talk about How We Write about Women Musicians." *Lockeland Springsteen.* Lockeland Springsteen, n.d. Web. 3 Aug. 2017.

4. Brie Schwartz. "Kelly Clarkson Can't Be Put Down: 'I'm Never Going to Obsess about My Body.'" *Redbook.* Hearst Communications, 14 Apr. 2015. Web. 3 Aug. 2017.

5. Jason Derulo. "Talk Dirty (feat. 2 Chainz)." *Google Play Music.* Google, n.d. Web. 3 Aug. 2017.

6. Leila Brillson. "File This under 'Obvious:' it's NOT Okay for Rick Ross to Rap about Date Rape." *Refinery29.* Refinery29, 28 Mar. 2013. Web. 3 Aug. 2017.

7. Nathan Hurst. "Sexual Objectification of Female Artists in Music Videos Exists Regardless of Race, MU Study Finds." *University of Missouri.* Curators of the University of Missouri, 4 Apr. 2012. Web. 3 Aug. 2017.

CHAPTER 5. WOMEN IN THE NEWS

1. "Global Media Monitoring Project 2015." *Who Makes the News?* Agility, n.d. Web. 3 Aug. 2017.

SOURCE NOTES
CONTINUED

2. Ibid.

3. Ibid.

4. "Global Media Monitoring Project 2015." *Who Makes the News?* Agility, n.d. Web. 14 Aug. 2017.

5. Where Voters Saw Most Sexist Treatment of Women Candidates in Media." *Women's Media Center.* Women's Media Center, 18 Nov. 2016. Web. 14 Aug. 2017.

6. Nina Bahadur. "Women in Politics: Coverage Focuses More on Personality Traits, Less on Issues, Study Finds." *Huffpost.* Oath, 8 July 2013. Web. 3 Aug. 2017.

7. Mattie Kahn. "What the Media Gets Wrong about Women in Politics." *Elle.* Hearst Communications, 28 Apr. 2015. Web. 3 Aug. 2017.

8. Kae Reynolds. "Clinton Finds Her Voice—But the Sexism That Greets Women's Speech Endures." *The Conversation.* The Conversation US, 29 July 2016. Web. 14 Aug. 2017.

9. Mattie Kahn. "What the Media Gets Wrong about Women in Politics." *Elle.* Hearst Communications, 28 Apr. 2015. Web. 14 Aug. 2017.

10. Ibid.

CHAPTER 6. WORKING IN THE MEDIA INDUSTRY

1. "WMC Divided 2015: The Media Gender Gap." *Women's Media Center.* Women's Media Center, n.d. Web. 14 Aug. 2017.

2. "The Status of Women in the U.S. Media 2015." *Women's Media Center.* Women's Media Center, n.d. Web. 14 Aug. 2017.

3. "ASNE Releases 2016 Diversity Survey Results." *ASNE.* American Society of News Editors, 9 Sept. 2016. Web. 14 Aug. 2017.

4. Ibid.

5. "The Status of Women in the U.S. Media 2017." *Women's Media Center.* Women's Media Center, n.d. Web. 14 Aug. 2017.

6. Anna Griffin. "Where Are the Women?" *Nieman Reports.* President and Fellows of Harvard College, 11 Sept. 2014. Web. 14 Aug. 2017.

7. Danielle Paquette. "Pay Doesn't Look the Same for Men and Women at Top Newspapers." *Washington Post.* Washington Post, 10 Mar. 2016. Web. 14 Aug. 2017.

8. "ASNE Releases 2016 Diversity Survey Results." *ASNE.* American Society of News Editors, 9 Sept. 2016. Web. 14 Aug. 2017.

9. Danielle Paquette. "Pay Doesn't Look the Same for Men and Women at Top Newspapers." *Washington Post.* Washington Post, 10 Mar. 2016. Web. 14 Aug. 2017.

10. Charlotte Alter. "Jill Abramson Insists on Calling Herself 'Fired.'" *Time.* Time, 17 July 2014. Web. 14 Aug. 2017.

11. Dr. Martha M. Lauzen. "The Celluloid Ceiling: Behind-the-Scenes Employment of Women on the Top 100, 250, and 500 Films of 2016." *Center for the Study of Women in Television & Film.* Dr. Martha Lauzen, n.d. Web. 14 Aug. 2017.

12. "New Research From Women's Media Center Concludes 'Media on All Platforms Are Failing Women.'" *Women and Hollywood.* Women and Hollywood, n.d. Web. 14 Aug. 2017.

13. Yvonne Villarreal, "Female TV Directors Make Modest Strides, but Minority Representation Drops, DGA Reports," *Los Angeles Times*. Los Angeles Times, 25 Aug. 2015. Web. 14 Aug. 2017.

CHAPTER 7. EFFECTS ON SOCIETY

1. Jason Lynch. "U.S. Adults Consume an Entire Hour More of Media Per Day Than They Did Just Last Year." *Adweek*. Adweek, 27 June 2016. Web. 14 Aug. 2017.

2. Ibid.

3. Kelly Wallace. "Teens Spend a 'Mind-Boggling' 9 Hours a Day Using Media, Report Says." *CNN*. Cable News Network, 3 Nov. 2015. Web. 14 Aug. 2017.

4. Ibid.

5. Ibid.

6. "Sexualization of Girls Is Linked to Common Mental Health Problems in Girls and Women—Eating Disorders, Low Self-Esteem, and Depression; An APA Task Force Reports." *American Psychological Association*. American Psychological Association, 19 Feb. 2007. Web. 14 Aug. 2017.

7. "Get the Facts on Eating Disorders." *NEDA*. National Eating Disorders Association, n.d. Web. 14 Aug. 2017.

8. "Afraid to Be Your Selfie? Survey Reveals Most People Photoshop Their Images." *Renfrew Center*. Renfrew Center, 20 Feb. 2014. Web. 14 Aug. 2017.

9. "Sexualization of Girls Is Linked to Common Mental Health Problems in Girls and Women—Eating Disorders, Low Self-Esteem, and Depression; An APA Task Force Reports." *American Psychological Association*. American Psychological Association, 19 Feb. 2007. Web. 14 Aug. 2017.

CHAPTER 8. WORKING FOR CHANGE IN THE MEDIA

1. Susanna Kim. "Children's Place Pulls 'Sexist' T-Shirt." *ABC News*. ABC News Internet Ventures, 6 Aug. 2013. Web. 14 Aug. 2017.

2. Ibid.

3. Emanuella Grinberg. "Sexist Super Bowl Ads? #NotBuyingIt, Some Say." *CNN*. Cable News Network, 5 Feb. 2013. Web. 14 Aug. 2017.

4. Andrew Pulver. "Reese Witherspoon Talks Up #AskHerMore on the Oscars Red Carpet." *Guardian*. Guardian News and Media Limited, 22 Feb. 2015. Web. 14 Aug. 2017.

5. Neha Prakash. "Victoria's Secret Quietly Changed Its 'Perfect Body' Slogan after Backlash." *Mashable*. Mashable, 7 Nov. 2014. Web. 14 Aug. 2017.

6. Ibid.

7. "The Super Bowl, Diversity and Inclusion Won." *Representation Project*. Representation Project, 7 Feb. 2017. Web. 14 Aug. 2017.

8. "Campaign Launch 'End News Media Sexism." *Who Makes the News?* Agility, 9 Dec. 2016. Web. 14 Aug. 2017.

9. Stephanie Goodman. "More Women Were Protagonists in 2016 Movies." *New York Times*. New York Times, 21 Feb. 2017. Web. 14 Aug. 2017.

10. Katie Hope. "Unilever to Use 'Less Sexist' Ads." *BBC News*. BBC, 22 June 2016. Web. 14 Aug. 2017.

INDEX

ABOUT THE AUTHOR

DUCHESS HARRIS, JD, PHD

Professor Harris is the chair of the American Studies Department at Macalester College. The author and coauthor of four books (*Hidden Human Computers: The Black Women of NASA* and *Black Lives Matter* with Sue Bradford Edwards, *Racially Writing the Republic: Racists, Race Rebels, and Transformations of American Identity* with Bruce Baum, and *Black Feminist Politics from Kennedy to Clinton/Obama*), she has been an associate editor for *Litigation News*, the American Bar Association Section's quarterly flagship publication, and was the first editor-in-chief of *Law Raza Journal*, an interactive online race and the law journal for William Mitchell College of Law.

She has earned a PhD in American Studies from the University of Minnesota and a Juris Doctorate from William Mitchell College of Law.